Teen Guide to Paying for College

Carla Mooney

San Diego, CA

About the Author
Carla Mooney is the author of many books for young adults and children.
She lives in Pittsburgh, Pennsylvania, with her husband and three children.

© 2017 ReferencePoint Press, Inc.
Printed in the United States

For more information, contact:
ReferencePoint Press, Inc.
PO Box 27779
San Diego, CA 92198
www.ReferencePointPress.com

Picture Credits:
Cover: Shutterstock.com/zimmytws
 4: Maury Aaseng
34: Shutterstock.com/Newnow
51: Depositphotos

LIBRARY OF CONGRESS CATALOGING-IN-PUBLICATION DATA

Names: Mooney, Carla, 1970- author.
Title: Teen guide to paying for college / by Carla Mooney.
Description: San Diego, CA : ReferencePoint Press, Inc., 2016. | Series: Teen guide to finances | Includes bibliographical references and index.
Identifiers: LCCN 2016013791 (print) | LCCN 2016018093 (ebook) | ISBN 9781682820841 (hardback) | ISBN 9781682820858 (eBook)
Subjects: LCSH: College costs--United States--Juvenile literature. | Student aid--United States--Juvenile literature.
Classification: LCC LB2342 .M585 2016 (print) | LCC LB2342 (ebook) | DDC 378.3/8--dc23
LC record available at https://lccn.loc.gov/2016013791

Contents

College Costs Are Rising

The cost of going to college in the United States has steadily risen since the 1990s. This is true for tuition and for combined tuition and room and board costs at both public and private (not-for-profit) four-year colleges.

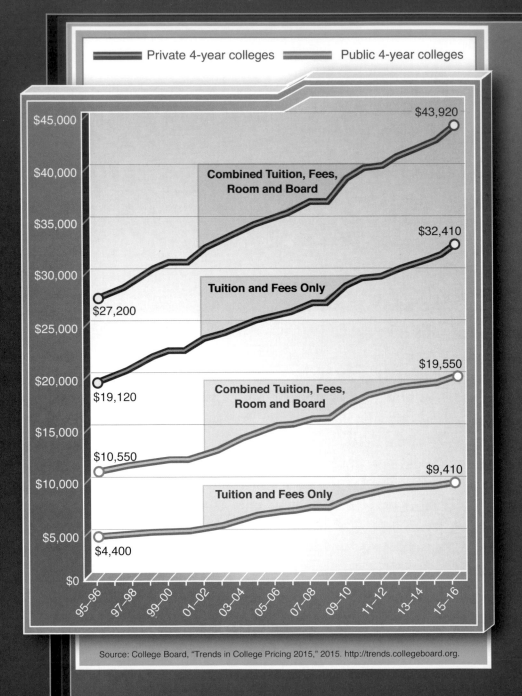

Source: College Board, "Trends in College Pricing 2015," 2015. http://trends.collegeboard.org.

Chapter One

The Cost of College

When Jamie and Cindy Harris started looking at colleges In 2013 for their oldest daughter, they were shocked at the price. The Florida family found that one year at elite schools such as Harvard or Princeton cost nearly $60,000 in tuition alone. Even at less expensive state schools, annual tuition ran about $20,000. "With three kids . . . by the time we're done, we're looking at over 800,000 dollars," Jamie Harris explained in a 2013 interview on the NBC (Miami) website.

The family's only option was financial aid. They applied for and received a package that included scholarships, grants, and a work-study job to help pay for their daughter's tuition and other costs at the University of Michigan. The couple says that without the financial aid package, they would not have been able to send their daughter to her dream school. They advise other families in the same situation to explore all of the options available for paying for college.

Rising Costs

As the Harris family discovered, the cost of college is higher than ever. According to the College Board, a

Work-Study Jobs

A federal work-study program provides part-time jobs to students while they are in school to help pay their education expenses. Vivian Warren, a senior psychology student at Nevada State College, has a work-study job to help pay college expenses. "Work study is an excellent way to supplement your college tuition," Warren said in a March 2014 interview on the *USA Today* website. "In combination with grants and scholarships, I do not have to worry about my college tuition getting paid." Warren says that her work-study job has several benefits in addition to the money she earns. Through her work-study job, she has networked and made contacts with students and professors on her campus. In addition, she has control of her schedule and the flexibility to manage it around her schoolwork. "I am able to work on campus and my work hours are scheduled around school. Each semester, I am able to change my hours to what works best for me. I can build my network, earn money and not have to worry about work affecting school," she said.

nonprofit organization that administers standardized tests and provides information about college admissions, the average published cost of tuition and fees (including room and board) at a private four-year university for the 2015–2016 school year was $43,920. Costs at a public four-year college are also expensive, with tuition, fees, and room and board averaging $19,550.

College costs can vary significantly from school to school. Factors such as a school's location, the types of degrees it offers, and whether it is a public or private two-year or four-year institution all affect cost. For example, in 2015–2016, tuition alone at Harvard University in

Massachusetts was $45,278. In contrast, in-state tuition for undergraduate students at Pennsylvania State University for the 2015–2016 school year was between $16,500 and $21,300, depending on the program of study.

Yet tuition is only one part of college costs. Students and their families are expected to pay other expenses, which can quickly add up to a significant amount of money. Students who live on campus must pay for room and board. According to the College Board, the average published cost of room and board alone for the 2015–2016 school year was $10,140 at four-year public universities and $11,510 at four-year private universities. Additionally, those who live at home and commute to campus pay travel costs. All students are expected to buy books and school supplies. Most schools also charge fees for activities, parking, and other campus services.

Financial Aid Can Help

In spite of rising costs, millions of students and their families believe that it is important to get a college degree. Yet paying for college is not easy for the average family. For many families, financial aid bridges the gap between what they can afford and the cost of college. According to the College Board, approximately two-thirds of full-time students pay for college with the help of grants and scholarships. Additionally, many students and their families also take out loans, with 37 percent of financial aid dollars being awarded as federal loans, according to the College Board.

Scott Nicks of Walker, Michigan, wanted to attend Central Michigan University (CMU), but money was tight for his family after the death of his father. His mother, Rachel, worried about how she was going to pay for college for Scott and his two younger brothers. She credits CMU's financial aid office with helping her and Scott find a way to pay for college through scholarships and grants. In an interview on the financial aid page of the state of Michigan's website, she advises students to not let cost stop them from going to college. She says, "A lot of students say they want to go to college but don't have money. After going through this process, I am now confident in saying that if you have the desire and the will to go to college, the money is there but you have to want it bad enough [and research] what is out there."

Types of Assistance

Students can get financial aid from a variety of sources. Federal and state governments offer financial assistance for college, as do some nonprofit organizations and private businesses.

The federal government has several financial aid programs for students. The US Department of Education awards about $150 billion a year in financial aid to more than 15 million students. This aid covers student expenses such as tuition, fees, room and board, books and supplies, transportation, and other school-related expenses. Grants, loans, and work-study programs are typical types of federal financial aid. A grant is often based on financial need and does not need to be repaid unless the student withdraws from school. Student loans are funded by the

> "If you have the desire and the will to go to college, the money is there but you have to want it bad enough [and research] what is out there."
>
> —Rachel, mother of a Central Michigan University student.

What's in a Name?

When saving for college, families should carefully consider the pros and cons of saving in a parent's name or a student's. Saving in a student's name offers some tax advantages because they are usually in a lower tax bracket than their parents. However, there are disadvantages if a student plans to apply for financial aid. Any assets in a student's name, like a savings account or investment account, is assessed at 20 percent. This means that the federal government and schools calculate that the student will pay 20 percent of his or her assets toward tuition. Parent assets are only assessed at a maximum rate of 5.65 percent. Thus, if a $40,000 college savings account is in the student's name, the college would expect the student to use 20 percent of the fund, or $8,000, to pay for the first year of college. However, if the same $40,000 fund is in the parent's name, the college would assess only 5.65 percent for the first year of college, which would amount to $2,260. This is just one of the many factors that go into calculations of financial assistance.

federal government, often at low interest rates, but need to be repaid with interest after graduation. Work-study programs provide part-time work for a student while he or she is enrolled in college to help pay expenses.

States, colleges, and nonprofit organizations are other sources of financial aid. Students who are not eligible for federal assistance may be able to get financial aid from the states in which they live—usually in the form of grants or loans. Many colleges also have financial aid programs, sometimes in the form of scholarships from specific departments. Additionally, many companies, nonprofits, and community groups offer scholarships to qualified students to help them pay for college. This money does not need to be repaid.

Christopher Gray, a student at Drexel University in Philadelphia, received a federal need-based grant to help pay for college. But the grant was limited to about $5,500 a year and did not cover all of his college costs. Because he was from a low-income family, Gray needed to find another source of money to pay for college. He started applying for scholarships the summer before his senior year of high school. "For me, it was either I apply for financial aid or I don't go. Scholarships were my only way out," he said in a November 2015 interview on the website of Fox8 in North Carolina. Gray eventually received more than thirty-five private scholarships, which gave him enough money to go to Drexel for free. Gray graduated in spring 2015 and has some scholarship money left over to help him pay for graduate school.

Aid Is Not Guaranteed

Getting financial aid to pay for college is not guaranteed. In fact, very few students receive full-tuition scholarships to college. According to the College Board, the typical full-time undergraduate student attending a four-year college receives assistance with less than half of his or her costs. When Barbara Constable's oldest son applied to college, he received $10,000 less in financial aid than his family could afford to pay. "I literally cried for three days when we got that first financial aid offer," said Constable in an April 2014 interview that appeared on the *New York Times* website. "I was in such shock, it took me three days to regain my composure and call them and say, 'How are we supposed to afford this?

You must be kidding.'" The family was forced to obtain loans to make up the difference.

In some cases, the lack of financial aid can derail a student's dreams of going to an elite college. Tracy Mayor, a Boston journalist, says that she and her son were initially thrilled when he was accepted to the prestigious institution he hoped to attend. When she pored through the acceptance packet, however, there was no mention of financial aid. Eventually she asked her son to e-mail the admissions office and ask if merit aid information would be coming later. "The answer comes back almost too quickly: If there was no mention of a merit scholarship in his acceptance letter, then he's not getting one," she wrote in April 2013 for the *Washington Post*. "And just like that, a yes becomes a no. Because tuition, room, board and fees at Selective U are $64,800. Per year. The $5,500 in federal student loans, which is what we can expect in financial aid, will put only the tiniest dent in that number. So, except for bragging rights, that school is off the list."

> "For me, it was either I apply for financial aid or I don't go."
>
> —*Christopher Gray, a Drexel University student.*

Start Saving Early

It is never too late to start saving for college. Paying for college is a lot easier if students and their families start saving early. According to the FinAid website, children born today will face tuition costs that are three to four times higher than they are now. The sooner a family starts saving for college, the more time their money will have to grow. For example, if a family invests $4,000 and earns interest of 6 percent annually, it will grow to

$4,240 in one year. Interest on savings can grow in a variety of other ways, which is why starting to save early has many benefits.

One of the most common ways to save for college is a 529 savings plan. Also known as qualified tuition programs, these plans allow savings to grow tax-free. The owner invests after-tax money into the plan and can withdraw the money and any investment earnings tax-free to use toward qualified college expenses such as tuition, fees, and room and board. Other savings plans that have tax advantages include Roth IRAs (Individual Retirement Accounts) and Coverdell education savings accounts.

Paying for college can be tough for students and families. For many, financial aid is the only way they can afford college costs. Understanding what types of aid are available and how to apply for them is the first step toward financing a college education. While the process may seem confusing, millions of students have learned how to navigate the financial aid system and have found a way to pay for college.

Chapter Two

Grants and Scholarships

Not all forms of financial aid are the same. Grants and scholarships are considered gift aid, which means that students do not have to pay the money back. Nor do they have to work in exchange for the funds. In addition, money received via grants and scholarships is usually tax-free. According to the College Board's *Trends in Student Aid 2015* report, grants made up 50 percent of all student aid for the 2014–2015 school year. These grants came from the federal government (37 percent), state governments (8 percent), colleges (41 percent), and private companies and organizations (14 percent). While government grants are based on need, grants from colleges, private companies, and organizations can be based on merit or a combination of both. For many students, grants and scholarships are just one piece of the financial aid pie, as they also use savings, loans, and other sources of money to pay for college.

Although the terms *grants* and *scholarships* are often used interchangeably, there are some differences between these two types of financial aid. Most grants are based on need. They are awarded based on a student's financial situation. In contrast, scholarships are often based on merit. This means that they are awarded to students who have demonstrated certain qualities, such as academic skills or athletic talent.

Federal Pell Grants

One of the most common grants used by students to pay for college is a government Pell Grant. According to the College Board, 8.2 million students received Pell Grants in 2014–2015, totaling $30.3 billion.

To receive a Pell Grant, a student must meet certain eligibility requirements. First, they must demonstrate financial need. The US Department of Education evaluates information submitted by students and families when they apply for a Pell Grant. They use this information to determine the expected family contribution (EFC)—which is the amount the government believes a family can afford to pay for college. The department then compares a student's EFC to the projected total cost of attending college, including tuition, room and board, books, and other fees. If the total cost of college exceeds the student's EFC, he or she is eligible for a Pell Grant.

Additionally, a student must have earned either a high school diploma or a general equivalency diploma or have finished a high school education in an approved home-school program. The student must be enrolled or accepted as an undergraduate student in an eligible college program. Students applying for a Pell Grant must

> "These scholarship opportunities have allowed me to accomplish many of my academic goals and even some of my life dreams."
>
> —Christopher Scott, a University of Toledo student and recipient of a Cleveland Foundation scholarship.

Scholarship Scams

Students looking for scholarships to pay for college should also be on the lookout for scholarship scams. Every year hundreds of thousands of students and parents lose money to such scams. Scammers often pretend to be legitimate government agencies, grant-giving foundations, education lenders, or scholarship-matching services and contact students by phone, mail, or e-mail. They typically have names that include words like *National*, *Federal*, *Foundation*, or *Administration* to make them seem legitimate.

Scholarship scams occur in many forms. Most require students and parents to pay money up front. They may characterize these payments as application fees, advance fees on a loan, or a redemption fee or taxes on a scholarship that the student has supposedly won. Other scams charge a fee for a scholarship-matching service that guarantees the student will win a scholarship or the company will refund the student's money. Scammers may simply take the money and disappear or make it virtually impossible to qualify for a refund.

Other scams are disguised as free financial aid seminars. In reality, these sessions are often designed as sales pitches for insurance, investment ideas, and financial aid consulting services. In order to avoid scams, students and parents should make sure they do their homework about each offer before they sign.

also be citizens of the United States or eligible noncitizens.

The maximum amount awarded via a Pell Grant was capped at $5,815 for the 2016–2017 school year. The actual amount a student receives depends on financial need and other factors. In 2014 the average Pell Grant award per student was $3,673.

Other Types of Grants

The Supplemental Education Opportunity Grant (SEOG) is another type of federal grant. Unlike the Pell Grant, the SEOG is administered by colleges. The federal government gives the schools a lump sum of grant money that they distribute to students. Awards under this grant typically run from $100 to $4,000 per student, per year.

Many colleges also award their own grants to students. Some schools award grants based on financial need, and others award merit-based grants. Unlike federal grants, there is no limit on the size of a college grant. These awards can range from a few hundred dollars to the entire cost of tuition.

Students who attend college in their home state or in a state with a reciprocal agreement may be eligible for a state grant. Administered by the states, these grants are usually based on need. The amount of tuition at the school a student attends also factors into the size of the grant. A student attending a local state university may receive a smaller grant than a similar student at a private college. The amounts of state grants can go as high as $6,000 per year.

Scholarships

Scholarships from colleges are the most common type of scholarships. Colleges often award their scholarships based on merit. Michelle Tallarita, a top high school senior, received one such merit-based scholarship in 2012. She was offered a $20,000 scholarship from Lafayette University in Easton, Pennsylvania. "My mom opened the letter and she called me and told me I got the . . . scholarship," Tallarita told National Public Radio in May

Scholarships Open Doors

When Greta Twombly was applying to college, she visited several campuses along the East Coast and fell in love with George Washington University in Washington, DC. She decided to apply to the school, although she knew that she needed financial assistance in order to afford the cost. When Twombly received her admissions acceptance, she was thrilled to learn that she had also been awarded a Presidential Academic Scholarship, which would pay for part of her tuition expenses. "It was the best thing that could have happened. Immediately, I felt a weight lift off my shoulders—it was such a welcoming feeling," she said in a March 2014 interview on the GW Alumni website. Twombly jumped into the university community immediately, joining several student groups and working in the admissions office during her junior and senior years. "The scholarship gave me time to really get involved in a way that I wouldn't have been able to otherwise," she says. After graduating in 2010, Twombly worked on political campaigns for several years and then took a position with the American Sustainable Business Council.

2012. "And she was like, 'It's a humongous scholarship!'" The sizable scholarship convinced Tallarita to enroll at Lafayette. Scholarships from colleges may also be awarded to students within a particular division or major within the school. For example, at Kenyon College in Gambier, Ohio, students who take courses in studio art are eligible for a scholarship, as are students involved in the school's music program.

Outside scholarships are those given to students by organizations or groups that are not affiliated with the college or government. These scholarships can come from foundations, companies, community organizations, and other private entities. Students may also find local scholarships sponsored by their church, synagogue, or other religious community; organizations such as the Rotary Club; employers; and community groups.

National outside scholarships include programs like the National Merit Scholarship Corporation, Gates Millennium Scholars, Intel Science Talent Search, and the Coca-Cola Scholars Foundation. Unlike local or state scholarships, which are limited to certain geographic areas, students across the country can apply for national scholarships. With so many students eligible to apply for this aid, the competition for these awards is often intense.

> "Both of my parents work, but they don't have degrees. We're not dying for money, but they don't have thousands of dollars every year for me to go to school."
>
> —Abbey Hayes, a recipient of Georgia's HOPE scholarship.

In Ohio, the Cleveland Foundation has awarded more than $47.6 million in scholarships to more than ten thousand students since 1987, primarily to students from northeastern Ohio. Christopher Scott is a recipient of $10,000 in Cleveland Foundation scholarships. He used that money to attend the University of Toledo, where he studied middle childhood education and earned a spot on the dean's list for good grades. He is the first member of his family to attend and graduate from college. He says that the foundation's help gave him the opportunity to further his education and give back to his community. "These scholarship opportunities have allowed me to accomplish many of my academic goals and even some of my life dreams," says Scott in an interview on the Cleveland Foundation website.

One way to learn about scholarships is by talking to high school guidance counselors. Another source of information is found online at the College Board website, for instance. To apply for an outside scholarship, students should expect to complete an application form, financial aid form, and essay.

Keeping Grants and Scholarships

Grants and scholarships are typically awarded on an annual basis. When a student wins one, he or she may have to follow certain rules. For example, the student may have to maintain a minimum grade point average (GPA) or active status on an athletic team in order to keep receiving the financial aid. Additionally, there is no guarantee that a student receiving a grant or scholarship for his or her first year of college will receive the same aid in future years. Each year tens of thousands of college sophomores, juniors, and seniors lose grants and scholarships that they had planned to use to pay for college.

As a freshman student at Georgia State, Abbey Hayes earned a full-tuition scholarship from Georgia's HOPE (Helping Outstanding Pupils Educationally) scholarship program based on her 3.2 GPA in high school. When her grades slipped during her freshman year below the scholarship's required B average, she no longer qualified for the HOPE money and lost her scholarship. Hayes's parents were forced to take out loans to pay her tuition. "Both of my parents work, but they don't have degrees," she said in January 2014 in *Atlanta Magazine*. "We're not dying for money, but they don't have thousands of dollars every year for me to go to school." Luckily, Hayes was able to improve her grades and regain her scholarship in her junior and senior years.

As Hayes discovered, students need to maintain their grade levels and stay out of trouble in order to keep their grants and scholarships. Many schools have a minimum GPA for financial aid, even for need-based grants. Many schools require at least a 2.0 GPA to qualify for any type of financial aid. Students can even lose a Pell Grant if they do not meet academic standards. Grades are even more important to retain merit-based scholarships, with higher GPA minimums. In addition, students hoping to renew grants and scholarships need to stay out of trouble and avoid any legal or academic violations. If a student is arrested for buying or selling drugs, he or she can be banned from the Pell Grant program.

Students who receive athletic scholarships must maintain their athletic status, along with meeting GPA requirements and following university rules. Because the majority of athletic scholarships are renewed annually, if a student-athlete gets injured or stops playing, he or she can lose the scholarship. In 2009 Kyle Hardrick arrived at the University of Oklahoma on a basketball scholarship. At practice, a 300-pound (136 kg) teammate fell on Hardrick's right leg and injured his knee. Although team doctors told Hardrick that the injury was not serious, he did not play in a single game that year. In January 2011 Hardrick was still experiencing pain in his knee. A magnetic resonance imaging test revealed a torn meniscus, and Hardrick underwent an operation to repair the damage. With his future ability to play in question, Oklahoma did not renew his scholarship.

When looking for financial aid, grants and scholarships should be at the top of every student's list. These are the most attractive types of financial aid because they do not need to be paid back. For every dollar in grants and scholarships, students can finance their college education without adding debt to their future.

Chapter Three

Student Loans

Sometimes grants, scholarships, and other forms of gift aid do not cover the full cost of college. Many students supplement grants, scholarships, and savings with student loans. During the 2014–2015 school year, students took out $95.9 million in federal student loans, according to the College Board's *Trends in Student Aid 2015* report. An additional $10.1 million in nonfederal loans were also taken out to pay for college. According to Ted Beck, the president and CEO of the National Endowment for Financial Education, student loans should only be taken out after all other financial options have been exhausted. "Loans should be the last piece used to finance your education, especially for undergraduate study," he said in an interview that appeared on the Fox Business website.

A student loan is money that the student borrows and must pay back with interest. Student loans are usually taken out by the student, often with preferential terms. For example, the interest rates charged on student loans are typically lower than those charged on regular loans. Additionally, many student loans do not charge interest while students are still in college, and students do not have to begin repayment until they have either graduated or left college. Parents sometimes take out loans in their own names to pay for their child's college expenses.

Typically, there are two types of student loans. Federal student loans are funded by the federal government. These loans typically have lower interest rates and more flexible repayment terms than private loans. Private student loans come from private lenders such as banks, credit unions, state agencies, or schools. Most financial aid experts recommend that students pursue federal loans before considering private loans. "They are cheaper, more available, and they have better repayment terms than private student loans," says financial aid expert Mark Kantrowitz in a 2013 interview that appeared on the *Forbes* website. The number of students using student loans to pay for college is increasing. According to an analysis of government data published in the *Wall Street Journal* in 2015, the average college graduate that year owed more than $35,000 in student loans, more than twice the amount owed by graduates in 1995. In addition, almost 71 percent of graduates who received bachelor's degrees in 2015 had taken out student loans, compared to less than 50 percent in 1995.

Financial aid experts recommend that students keep their loan balances as low as possible. The more money one borrows, the higher the monthly loan payments after graduation. In order not to overburden themselves when it is time to repay student loans, students should consider their degree and job prospects after graduation.

"It's a good idea for parents and students to consider what the total debt will be after graduation."

—Haley Chitty, director of the National Association of Student Financial Aid Administrators.

"It's a good idea for parents and students to consider what the total debt will be after graduation, that they get a sense of how much the payments will likely be and the total interest owed and accrued depending on how they pay off the loan," says Haley Chitty, director of the National Association of Student Financial Aid Administrators, in an interview on the Fox Business website.

For most students and families, federal student loans are the best option. The interest rates on these loans are generally fixed, which eliminates increasing payments if rates go up in the future. In some cases, the government will subsidize the loan, meaning it will pay the interest on the loan while the student is still in school.

Federal Direct Loans

Federal direct loans, formerly known as federal Stafford loans, are the largest source of low-interest student loans. Under this program, the loan can be either subsidized or unsubsidized. Subsidized loans are awarded to undergraduate students based on need as determined by the Free Application for Federal Student Aid (FAFSA). Interest does not accrue on the loan until the student graduates, leaves college, or goes below half-time attendance status. Federal direct subsidized loans also generally have a lower interest rate than other loans.

Unsubsidized loans, known as federal direct unsubsidized loans, are available to both undergraduate and graduate students, regardless of need. The college determines the amount of the loan based on a student's college costs and other financial aid received. Unlike the subsidized loan, interest accrues on this type of loan while the student is still in school. Students are responsible for paying interest on the loan while in school or deferring

Evaluating Loans

Before taking out a loan, students and parents should carefully consider the terms of the loan, making sure that it is right for their situation. The following is a list of some questions to ask when evaluating a loan:

- What is the loan's interest rate?
- Is the interest rate fixed or variable?
- How will the loan be repaid? Over what period?
- Are there any loan fees?
- Can the loan's interest be deducted for tax purposes?
- Is the loan in the student's name or a parent's name?
- Does the loan require a cosigner?
- Is the loan secured or unsecured?

Borrowing can lead to high levels of debt that will be difficult to repay after college. By carefully evaluating student loans, students and families will be in the best position to make smart decisions for current and future needs.

the interest payments until they begin to repay the principal of the loan. Typically, all students who fill out a FAFSA are eligible to receive a federal direct unsubsidized loan.

There are borrowing limits on federal direct loans, depending on a student's year in college. Dependent students can borrow up to $5,500 for their freshman year, $6,500 for their sophomore year, and $7,500 for their junior and senior years. In each year, $2,000 of that amount must be unsubsidized.

The PLUS Option

Parents can also take out loans to pay for their child's college education. Known as a Parent Loan for Undergraduate Students (PLUS), these loans are designed to help parents who do not have the available cash to pay for college costs. Funded by the US Department of Education, this loan makes up the difference between college costs and the financial aid that a student has already received. As this loan is not based on need, almost any parent can apply for and receive a PLUS, provided he or she has a good credit history. Unlike other student loans, this type of loan is taken out by parents, not students. Parents are financially responsible for the loan and its repayment. Parents can borrow up to the annual total cost of attending college less any financial aid already received.

Parents with a shaky credit history or a recent bankruptcy may have difficulty getting a PLUS. This is what happened to one family. The son was accepted at the University of Maryland. The father, who spoke with the *U.S. News & World Report* in June 2015 but declined to be named, had applied for a PLUS. However, because the father had previously filed for bankruptcy, he failed the required credit check and was denied the loan. Without the loan, the father says, he did not know how he would pay for his son's college costs. Ultimately he appealed—and won—and his son was able to attend college. "I didn't know any other avenues if I was going to be turned down completely," the man said. "Fortunately, it all worked out."

Private Student Loans

After counting grants, scholarships, and government loans, students may need additional money to cover the cost of college. Private student loans can help fund the difference between the cost of college and the amount of money a student receives in financial aid and

Too Much Debt?

When Mallory Bayers graduated in 2013 with a music business degree from Full Sail University in Winter Park, Florida, she had accumulated $85,000 in student loans. Unable to get a job in her field, she works at a restaurant in Austin, Texas. Her monthly student loan payments were set at $900, but she had them reduced to $55 because she can barely afford to pay her bills on her current salary. Bayers realizes now that her student loan debt is holding her back. "If I were in debt for half as much, I would still say it was too much debt," said Bayers in an August 2014 interview on the *USA Today* website. "It's going to take half my life to pay all this money back for a degree I haven't exactly put to work yet." Bayers wishes that she had done more to avoid taking out so many loans when she was in school. "I would have educated myself on student loans for sure. I only applied for one scholarship when I know I could've applied for a lot more. I also would have applied for some internships while I was still in school."

government loans. Private lenders such as banks, credit unions, and other financial institutions offer students and parents private loans for college.

There are many different private loan options, each with different interest rates and fees. Typically, private loans have higher costs than federal student loans. They may also require a cosigner. Students can generally borrow larger amounts from a private lender than they can from federal loans. However, these loans have several disadvantages. Interest rates are typically variable, which means they can change over time and potentially increase payments. Even a private loan with a low interest rate may have high fees that cause the loan to cost more overall than another type of loan. Private loans are generally less flexible than federal loans if a student has trouble making payments.

Considering these drawbacks, most financial aid experts recommend that students attempt to use other sources of funding to pay for college before turning to private student loans. In a July 2013 interview on the *Forbes* website, student-loan consultant Heather Jarvis explained that she advises students to make private loans a last resort for college funding:

> Private student loans are typically more expensive and risky for student-loan borrowers because they lack the borrower protections and flexible repayment provisions of federal student loans. And although some borrowers with excellent credit might find private loans with lower interest rates, those rates are often variable and are almost certain to go up over time—sometimes without any cap. Additionally, the most generous debt-relief programs, like income-based repayment and public-service loan forgiveness, are only available to recipients of federal student loans.

Take On Debt Carefully

The decision to take on student loan debt should not be taken lightly. For some families, the costs of student loans are too high. In the spring of 2015, Patrick Walsh, a high school senior from Georgia, was accepted into two of his top schools, Stony Brook University and St. John's University, both in New York. Yet the financial aid packages he received required his family to come up with $25,000 each year to pay for his college costs. His parents, who both had good jobs and a take-home pay of about $75,000 annually, said they could not afford to put one-third of their income toward college costs. Walsh's father, John, insisted that his son not go into debt to pay for his dream school. "The economy being what it is, the jobs you're getting, it just doesn't seem worth that $90,000 burden on your shoulders. We weren't going to take more debt on us," said John Walsh in a May 2015 interview on the CNN Money website. Although the decision frustrated him, Patrick agreed and decided to attend a less expensive college.

> **"Debt is not to be taken lightly—it has significant and lasting consequences."**
>
> *—Heather Jarvis, student loan consultant.*

Student-loan consultant Jarvis advises students to carefully consider whether to take on debt to pay for college. In addition, Jarvis strongly recommends that students not borrow more than they expect to earn in their first year after graduation. "Debt is not to be taken lightly—it has significant and lasting consequences. However, education is highly valuable and arguably more important than ever—people with post-secondary degrees continue to have lower rates of unemployment and higher earnings over time," she said in a July 2013 interview on *Forbes*. "Of course, for many Americans, higher education is impossible without taking on debt, so I encourage clients to carefully consider what they can afford, borrow only what's necessary, and look at federal loans first."

Chapter Four

The Application Process

Every year millions of students apply for financial aid to help pay for college. Mandy Stango remembers feeling confused and unprepared when she and her family started applying for financial aid when she was a high school senior. The confusion began when they sat down to complete the Free Application for Federal Student Aid (FAFSA). "I sat there, I read the directions, and crossed my fingers and hoped I was doing the right thing," said Stango, now twenty-three, in an August 2014 interview on the National Public Radio website.

The FAFSA form is a critical step in applying for financial aid as students cannot qualify for either need-based or merit-based aid from schools without one on file. The form has more than one hundred questions that determine a student's eligibility for financial aid. Like millions of applicants, Stango and her family found the form intimidating and confusing. "It was asking for all sorts of terminologies that, as an 18-year-old, I hadn't encountered and didn't really understand," said Stango. "I remember just putting things in the different boxes based on what they instructed me to do, and just being like, well, I hope this is right." Although the process was confusing, Stango and her family completed the form, qualifying her to receive some financial aid.

Financial Aid Forms

Like Stango, all students must submit a FAFSA form in order to qualify for most financial aid, whether it is coming from the government or directly from colleges. The FAFSA must be filled out each year that a student is in college and applying for financial aid. Online, the form takes an average of fifty-five minutes to complete.

The FAFSA asks a variety of questions about a family's financial situation. The questions gather financial and personal information, such as how much money the student's parents earned in the previous year, what assets they own, and their marital status. The answers are used to determine how much money a family can contribute toward a student's college costs. That amount directly influences how much money, if any, a student might qualify for in terms of financial aid.

In addition to the FAFSA, students may need to complete a few other financial aid forms. Many private colleges and some state schools require students to fill out the CSS Profile (College Scholarship Service Profile). A few schools, particularly selective private colleges, require students to fill out their own financial aid forms. In order to be certain

> "A lot of parents feel they won't qualify. They want to know what that hard-and-fast income number is in order to qualify for financial aid, and there never is a hard-and-fast number."
>
> —Cora Manuel, an assistant financial aid director at Saint Mary's College of California.

what forms are required for a particular school, students should talk to the school's financial aid office.

Qualifying for Financial Aid

Most students qualify for some sort of financial aid. According to the US Department of Education, more than $150 billion of financial aid is given to college students each year. To get some of that money for college, students must meet eligibility requirements. They must be US citizens or eligible noncitizens (which usually means a person who has a green card). They must have either graduated from high school, earned a general equivalency diploma, or completed an approved high school home-school program. They must also be enrolled in an eligible degree or certificate program at a college or career school.

Financial aid forms like the FAFSA are used to determine the minimum amount a family is expected to pay for college costs, an amount called the expected family contribution (EFC). The EFC calculation is based on the assets and income of both the student and his or her parents. It measures the financial strength of a family and considers factors such as family income, certain investment assets, the size of the family, and whether there are any other students in college.

A student's eligibility for need-based financial aid is determined by taking the total cost of college and subtracting the EFC. If a student's EFC is less than the cost of college, then the student is eligible for need-based financial aid. Once a student has been admitted to a college, the financial aid office puts together an aid package made up of grants, work-study programs, and loans that will make up the difference between the EFC and the cost of college.

Each college has its own formula for determining aid, so a student may be asked to pay more or less money at different schools. In addition, although a student may be eligible for need-based financial aid, there is no guarantee that he or she will receive the amount needed to pay for school. When this occurs, the student or parents may have to take out private loans or work part-time to come up with the additional money needed.

Jessycas Simerly says that for most of her life, money has been a worry. Living with a single mom and her brother, the family scraped by, and Simerly did not think she could afford college. Then, as a high school senior,

A Costly Mistake

Many families make mistakes when filling out the FAFSA for the first time, leaving out important information or mislabeling it. For some, these mistakes can have significant consequences. Before her freshman year at Indiana University, Meredith Moon experienced this problem. When filling out the form, Moon and her parents incorrectly stated her stepfather's tax information. That error led to Moon receiving no financial aid her freshman year. "I was really worried I was going to have to drop out of school," said Moon in an August 2014 interview on the National Public Radio website. "That was an honest mistake, and it almost had me out of school the first semester." Moon says that her high school never discussed how to fill out these financial forms. "They were like, 'This is your parents' responsibility, this is something your parents should do,'" she says. "But when your parents haven't done this before? They tell you to do this, do this, do this, but they don't tell you what information you need or why."

she learned about financial aid to help pay for college. She applied to several colleges in her home state of Tennessee and was accepted into Tusculum College. "I filled out my FAFSA and was thrilled when I got the letter from [the college] telling me I'd been awarded scholarships and grants that covered most of my tuition. I qualified for a few loans as well, and decided to accept them," she says in an article on the Student Aid Alliance website.

Biggest Mistake: Not Filling Out the FAFSA

Financial aid experts say that one of the biggest mistakes students can make is not filling out the FAFSA. Some choose not to fill out the application because they believe that their parents' income or assets are too high to qualify for aid. "A lot of parents feel they won't qualify," says Cora Manuel, an assistant financial aid director at Saint Mary's College of California, in an article on the personal finance site NerdWallet in January 2016. "They want to know what that hard-and-fast income number is in order to qualify for financial aid, and there never is a hard-and-fast number because of the different variables that determine expected family contribution." According to aid experts, not filling out the form is a costly mistake.

By not filling out the FAFSA, students are very likely missing out on money they could have used to help pay for college. According to a study published in January 2016 by NerdWallet, high school graduates lost out on as much as $2.7 billion in financial aid during the 2014–2015 academic year. The study found that, in 2014, 1.4 million high school graduates skipped filling out the FAFSA, with almost 750,000 of them being eligible for a Pell Grant. "Everyone should complete the FAFSA," said

Mark Kantrowitz, an expert on student financial aid in an October 2015 interview on the Think Advisor website. "You can't get money if you don't apply, so always apply. Even if you don't qualify for aid, FAFSA is a prerequisite for unsubsidized federal Stafford loans and federal PLUS loans, which are available without regard to financial aid."

Financial Aid Deadlines

The FAFSA and other financial aid forms have strict deadlines that vary by form, college, and state. Sometimes these deadlines can be confusing. For example, the federal government has one deadline, but many states and colleges have earlier deadlines. Additionally, the CSS Profile may have a different deadline than the FAFSA for a specific school. Students are responsible for knowing which forms are required and what the filing due dates are. Students should check with their individual state and school financial aid websites to find out their requirements and deadlines for submitting financial aid forms. Because there are so many deadlines, many experts recommend that students create a chart or calendar to keep track of all due dates.

In addition, several schools have supplemental financial aid forms that students are required to complete in addition to the FAFSA or the CSS Profile. Supplemental aid forms should be sent directly to the requesting colleges. Individual aid forms may have different deadlines than standardized aid forms like the FAFSA.

When it comes to the FAFSA, It pays to be an early filer. Financial aid experts say that those who submit their forms early are more likely to get larger amounts of financial aid. "Students who file the FAFSA in January, February and March get more than twice as much grant funding, on average, as students who file the FAFSA later. This Is because many state and college aid programs have very early deadlines," wrote financial aid expert Kantrowitz in a 2015 article on the *Washington Post* website. Many schools award financial aid on a rolling basis, which means that they evaluate and award money in the order they receive applications. Having the FAFSA in early means that a student is one of the first in line for financial aid and has a better chance of receiving an award before a school runs out of money.

> "Everyone should complete the FAFSA. You can't get money if you don't apply, so always apply."
>
> —Mark Kantrowitz, a student financial aid expert.

Starting in the 2017–2018 school year, students and families can fill out the FAFSA as early as October 1 for the following school year. By taking advantage of the earlier submission date, students will now be able to get an idea of their financial aid eligibility before they apply to schools. In addition, students will be able to use filed income tax information from two prior tax years. This change will make it more likely that families will have accurate tax information available when filling out the form instead of trying to estimate numbers from a tax return that they have not yet filed with the IRS.

Missing the Deadline

Missing a financial aid deadline can be a very costly mistake. Colleges and states often have priority deadlines for financial aid, and applications received by these deadlines are given priority. Some states and colleges will award aid after the priority deadline, but students may receive lower awards. If a student misses the federal deadline, he or she is no longer eligible to submit the FAFSA for that year and will have to wait until the following year to submit. In a January 2014 article in the Huffington Post, W. Kent Barnds, the executive vice president of Augustana College in Rock Island, Illinois, commented,

> "The simple fact is that many funding agencies/institutions use deadlines to determine who receives funds and who does not, regardless of need eligibility."
>
> —W. Kent Barnds, executive vice president of Augustana College in Rock Island, Illinois.

The simple fact is that many funding agencies/institutions use deadlines to determine who receives funds and who does not, regardless of need eligibility. Frequently the FAFSA submission date is a key factor in determining eligibility for need-based awards, and missing a deadline by just a day can mean the difference in attending your dream school or being faced with unmet financial need.

Louisa, a sophomore at a private Texas college, was shocked when she opened her financial aid award letter at the beginning of the school year. The amount she was awarded was approximately $10,000 less than she had received the previous year. When she investigated, Louisa found out that her aid was decreased because her father had not sent in the financial aid paperwork until March. By the time her school received it, they had

Common Application Mistakes

Every year thousands of students make mistakes on their financial aid application. These mistakes hold up a student's application, potentially costing the student thousands of dollars in financial aid. According to Stacey Kostel, the director of admissions at the University of Illinois at Urbana-Champaign, the most common mistakes she sees on the FAFSA could be avoided by more carefully following directions. According to Kostel, these are common mistakes:

- Failing to correctly enter the student's legal name (not a nickname), Social Security number, and birth date.
- Submitting the form without entering the personal identification number for the student and parent, which serves as an electronic signature.
- Failing to answer all of the form's questions correctly and completely.
- Not updating the family's financial information if it was based on an estimate at the time of filing.

already awarded their supply of grant money. "It was awful," says Louisa in an article on the CollegeXpress website. "I still received my government loans, but the grants were the only reason I was able to come to this school in the first place." Louisa's parents were able to get bank loans to cover the missing aid, but it saddled them with debt that they had not anticipated. The following year Louisa's father made sure to submit all the financial aid forms by the second week of January. The mix-up almost derailed Louisa's college education. "I almost missed out on finishing my education because of that slip-up," she says.

Every year millions of students apply for financial aid. For many, the process is confusing and overwhelming. Students who file the wrong forms or wait too long may miss out on thousands of dollars in aid. Understanding how the application process works can help students and their families avoid financial aid pitfalls and get the money they need for school.

Chapter Five

Other Ways to Lower College Costs

When Alec Beland graduated from high school, he considered attending a private four-year university in Maine. But the cost seemed incredibly steep, even with financial aid, so Beland chose a different path to getting his degree. He enrolled at Southern Maine Community College (SMCC) to study precision manufacturing. "I figured I could go off to some private four-year college and be crazy in debt, or I could come to community college for two years," says Beland in an April 2015 interview with Maine's *Portland Press Herald* newspaper. In May 2015 Beland graduated with a two-year degree and transferred to the University of Southern Maine (USM) to earn a bachelor of science degree in technology management. Additionally, attending community college allowed Beland to work while in school, and his employer is reimbursing him for tuition, books, and lab fees at both SMCC and USM. When he graduates from USM, Beland will earn a bachelor's degree and will only have to pay back about $3,000 in student loans. If he had gone to the private four-year college he originally planned to attend, the tuition alone would have been $100,000 — and his debts would have been huge.

Most students who apply for financial aid do not get enough money to pay for all of their college costs. Students and their families are forced to come up with the difference, whether by taking out loans, working two jobs, or finding other sources of money. Some students, like Beland, consider creative strategies to lower the cost of college altogether. While some of these options are not the typical four-year college experience, they might enable a student to get the college degree he or she wants without losing his or her financial stability.

Attend Community College First

The cost of attending community college can be significantly cheaper than traditional four-year public universities. Some students choose to attend a community college for two years and then transfer to a four-year college to finish their bachelor's degree. This strategy is sometimes called a 2+2 plan. With careful planning, students can take many of their general core courses at a community college and then transfer their credits to a four-year public university. The student's diploma and degree will be from the four-year university but at a significantly lower expense. In addition to saving on tuition, students can attend school close to home, saving additional money on room and board.

Using a 2+2 strategy can significantly cut total college costs. For

> "I figured I could go off to some private four-year college and be crazy in debt, or I could come to community college for two years."
>
> —Alec Beland, a student who received a degree after attending two years of community college and two years at a university.

40

example, the national average for tuition for one year at a four-year public university in 2015 was $19,550, according to the College Board. Average tuition at a community college was $9,308 per year. Using these prices, tuition at a four-year university would cost $78,200. Under the 2+2 plan, the cost drops significantly to $57,716, which can be lowered further with financial aid.

Many states have guaranteed admission agreements between the state's community colleges and select four-year public universities. These agreements detail which universities guarantee admission to students who earn an associate's degree at a participating community college. They also detail which credits transfer. In the case of highly competitive state universities, the guaranteed admission that comes with a community college degree can be an advantage for students.

Yet not all colleges accept transfer credits from community colleges. Therefore, students should talk to advisers at both the community college and the four-year university in order to make sure they will get credit for the classes they have taken at the community college. If students discover too late that the university will not accept the transfer credits, they will not have saved any money at all.

Condense Time Spent in College

Most students enroll in college and expect to graduate in four years. Yet many students take longer than expected to finish their degree. According to a 2014 report from Complete College America, an Indianapolis-based nonprofit, only 19 percent of full-time students at most public universities earn a bachelor's degree in four years. Even at selective state universities, only 36

Going to College in Canada

For some students, going to college in Canada makes financial sense. Canadian colleges typically offer an excellent education for an affordable price. Twenty-three-year-old Eric Andreasen is a political science major from Portland, Maine, who chose to attend McGill University in Montreal. When Andreasen was choosing a college, he applied to several schools in the United States and Canada, eventually narrowing down his choices to either George Washington University in Washington, DC, or McGill in Canada. McGill offered him a full four-year education for the same cost of one year at George Washington. "When the financial packages came in, it was a no-brainer for me," Andreasen said in an online interview with NBC News on April 24, 2013. "I'm coming out with minimal debt," said Andreasen. "It brightens up the prospect of the future for me." Other students are making the same choice. According to the Institute for College Access & Success, 6 percent of McGill's student body is from the United States. In addition, the number of Americans who attend Canadian colleges has increased 50 percent since about 2003.

percent of full-time students finish their degree in four years.

Repeating classes because of poor grades or changing a major midstream can lengthen the amount of time a student spends in college. It will also take longer to graduate if a student takes too few credits per semester or is unable to register for required courses. According to the Complete College America report, the extra time in school costs students and their parents billions of dollars. The report continues: "Hands down, our best strategy to make college more affordable and a sure way to boost graduation rates over all is to ensure that many more students graduate on time."

Because every semester spent in school costs money, students who focus on completing their degree requirements in the least amount of time possible can lower their cost of college. To do this, students can use several strategies. In high school, taking advanced placement (AP) courses and getting a required minimum score on AP exams, enrolling in dual-credit courses, or passing College-Level Examination Program tests can all earn college credits before a student even begins college. In addition, college students can earn additional credits by attending summer school, which reduces the time needed to complete a degree. Many schools offer discounts on tuition to entice students to enroll in summer sessions. For example, at Indiana University, students received a 25 percent tuition discount during the summer.

In 2008, when Michaela Kron was a freshman at New York University (NYU), she already had earned a few college credits. Kron earned high scores on several AP exams and tested out of several introductory classes at NYU. "I realized that I could arrange my schedule so that if I took a couple of summer courses, I could graduate a year early and save a ton of money," she said in a May 2015 interview on the *U.S. News & World Report* website. The strategy saved her more than $41,000 in tuition and fees.

> "I realized that I could arrange my schedule so that if I took a couple of summer courses, I could graduate a year early and save a ton of money."
>
> —Michaela Kron, a New York University student.

Co-Op Education

Enrolling in a cooperative (co-op) education program can also reduce the cost of college. A co-op program combines classroom instruction with practical work experience. Students alternate between semesters in class and semesters of paid work at internships. Although these programs generally take about five years to complete and earn a degree, students earn money during their internships that can be used to offset college costs.

Students who attend Drexel University in Philadelphia participate in one of the country's largest college co-op programs. At Drexel, freshmen attend classes full-time. Then, depending on their major and program, they alternate six-month periods of classroom study with full-time employment with a co-op employer. Employers who take part in this program include Amazon, NBC Universal, and JP Morgan. Biology major Dania Jacubovich worked on a six-month pediatrics and gynecology co-op job at the Hospital de Clinicas, a teaching hospital located in Buenos Aires, Argentina. She assisted residents at the hospital and spent hours checking patients and speaking with their families. In an interview on the Drexel University website, Jacubovich says the co-op provided her with valuable firsthand experience that will help her in her future career as a doctor. "Everything that I see and experience is new to me. The amount of knowledge that I've gained is amazing," she says.

Join the Military

Under the Reserve Officers' Training Corps (ROTC) scholarship program, students can go to college for free in exchange for a period of required active-duty service in the US military after graduation. Northeastern University graduate Alixandra Powers was a cadet in the school's Army ROTC program. The ROTC program paid her tuition, more than $39,000 annually, plus additional money for other living expenses. "It covers all the costs. I've never paid a cent to go to Northeastern. It's really nice," Powers said in a 2013 interview that appeared on Boston's Fox25 news website. Students interested in this option can apply for an ROTC scholarship during their junior or senior year of high school. All branches of the military provide ROTC scholarships that cover the cost of tuition, fees, books, and living expenses. Alternately, students who enlist in the military out of high school can later attend college with assistance. Military veterans who serve at least thirty-six months of active duty receive financial assistance for school that includes thirty-six months of tuition and fees, a housing allowance, and a stipend for books and supplies.

> "When I graduated from high school, I made the decision to take a year off from school and just work full time and save up money so that I might not have to take out a lot of loans to pay for school."
>
> —Sarah Swainson, a student at Tennessee's Chattanooga State Community College.

Top-performing students can apply for admission to one of the military service academies, such as the US Naval Academy, the US Military Academy, or the US Air Force Academy. Admission to these institutions is highly competitive, and candidates need to be nominated by either a member of Congress or the vice president of the United States. While tuition is free, students are required to serve at least five years in active-duty military service after graduation.

Take Time Off to Work

Although most high school graduates want to attend college right away, some wait a year before enrolling in college. Instead, they work full-time and save money. Having this additional savings can reduce the amount of loans students need to pay for college, decreasing interest costs over time. Students who choose to defer enrollment can apply to colleges at the same time as

Online Learning

Many colleges are in the process of expanding opportunities for students to take courses online. Going online for a year or more can save students money in several ways. A student who takes a year of online classes and lives at home eliminates room and board fees, which can save thousands of dollars in one semester. In addition, online classes eliminate the need to pay for travel expenses to and from a college campus. Most online classes present the material in a downloadable form, eliminating the need to purchase expensive textbooks and supplies, which can save students hundreds of dollars each semester. Additionally, online learners typically earn their degree in less time than those who attend a traditional campus, which saves on tuition costs.

Online learning is not for everyone, though. Students who are easily distracted, need contact with other students and teachers, or have difficulty self-motivating may not do well in this type of program. However, for students who are focused and self-motivated, pursuing a degree through an online college can easily save thousands of dollars each semester. This savings, along with the convenience and flexibility of online learning, is driving more people to enroll in online colleges.

the rest of their high school classmates but then ask for a one-year deferment once they are accepted. "When I graduated from high school, I made the decision to take a year off from school and just work full time and save up money so that I might not have to take out a lot of loans to pay for school," explains Sarah Swainson, a student at Tennessee's Chattanooga State Community College, in the January 27, 2016, issue of the *U.S. News & World Report*. "During my one year of work I was able to save up enough to cover my college tuition, and I'm also still working part time to continue building my savings. So while I may not have graduated debt-free yet, I am fairly certain that I will be able to obtain this goal, and hopefully even have some money left over."

When financial aid is not enough to cover the cost of college, turning to nontraditional strategies to lower college's overall cost can make an education affordable. While some of these strategies are not the typical four-year college experience, they enable students to earn the degree they want, at a price they can afford.

Chapter Six

Managing College Debt

Once students graduate from college, they need to be prepared to start paying back any loans they took out for school. About 70 percent of 2015 graduates had student loan debt, according to an analysis that year by Mark Kantrowitz, a financial aid expert and publisher of Edvisors, a website that gives information about college costs and financial aid. The average student graduated with $35,051 in student debt, according to the same analysis.

In fact, student loans are the country's second largest consumer debt market, and the numbers are staggering. As of 2015 there were more than 40 million federal and private student loan borrowers. Together, they owed more than $1.2 trillion, according to the Consumer Financial Protection Bureau, a government agency that deals with consumer finance markets. Many of these borrowers are struggling to keep up with their monthly loan payments. Knowing how to manage college debt can help these borrowers avoid payment pitfalls.

Paying Off Loans

Graduation starts the clock ticking on student loan payments. Government loans generally give students a six-month grace period before requiring payments. This grace period allows students time to find a job and start earning and saving money. Even so, paying off student loans is not as simple as it sounds. There are several different repayment programs along with opportunities to postpone payment. However, if students defer payment or negotiate lower payments over a longer period of time, interest still accrues on the debt, sometimes adding thousands of dollars to the loan. As a result, the longer students take to pay off loans, the more interest will accrue and the more the debt will cost them overall.

Megan Richardson graduated from East Carolina University with nearly $35,000 in student loans, along with car payments and other bills. She repaid her loans within two years by cutting back on expenses and being extremely careful with her money. She moved back in with her parents to save money on rent, used coupons, and budgeted every penny that she spent. Richardson took the money she saved and put it toward repaying her student loans. "Each month, I overpaid on every loan I had in order to pay off the debt sooner and decrease the amount of interest I accumulated. It was a very long two years and I felt extremely broke for the entire time, but all of the lifestyle changes I made allowed me to pay off all of my debt in those two years," she said in an interview with the *U.S. News & World Report* on January 27, 2016.

> "Each month, I overpaid on every loan I had in order to pay off the debt sooner and decrease the amount of interest I accumulated."
>
> —Megan Richardson, graduate of East Carolina University.

Federal Repayment Programs

For students with federal loans, the government's standard repayment plan is the simplest one for loan repayment. Under this plan, loans are repaid in equal installments over a ten-year period. While the monthly payments may be higher under the standard plan as compared to other plans, borrowers will generally pay less interest over the life of the loans than with other repayment plans. If a student is unable to make higher monthly payments, they may choose a repayment program that stretches repayment over a longer period. Although the longer-term plan has lower monthly payments, the borrower will pay more interest over the life of the loan, making the total loan cost more expensive.

When student loan payments are high compared to income, some borrowers choose an income-driven repayment plan. Typically, the payment amount under an income-driven repayment plan is calculated as a percentage of the student's income. This keeps payments low because many students do not earn a lot of money while still in school. The trade-off, however, is that with lower monthly payments or a longer repayment period, the borrower will generally pay more interest over the life of the loan. This sometimes adds up to a substantial amount.

Cameron Diggs, a 2015 graduate of Georgetown University in Washington, DC, says that when she was deciding what repayment plan to choose, she studied the descriptions of each type of repayment plan on her loan servicer's website. She ultimately decided on a repayment plan that had manageable payments.

With several options available, students can choose the repayment plan that best fits their circumstances.

If circumstances change and another repayment program becomes a better fit, students can switch payment plans at any time.

Loan Consolidation

Students with multiple federal student loans can simplify the repayment process by consolidating all of their loans into one large loan. Monthly loan payments can also be lowered by extending the repayment period up to thirty years. However, the longer repayment period means the borrower will pay more in interest costs over the life of the loan. Only government loans are eligible to be consolidated; private loans from colleges or other institutions cannot be combined in the federal consolidated program.

Ian Foss, a policy liaison with the US Department of Education, says that loan consolidation was the right

Young college graduates proudly hold their diplomas on graduation day. Graduation starts the clock ticking on repayment of student loans, although government loans generally give students a few months to find a job and start earning money.

Learning Financial Responsibility

When Hadley Malcolm graduated in 2011, she owed $25,000 in student loans. By 2016 she had worked the outstanding balance down to about $13,000 and expected to pay off the rest within three years. Malcolm says that having debt has had an unexpected silver lining: it has forced her to learn financial responsibility. She tracks every dollar she spends and sometimes says no to dinners with friends or exotic vacations. She has learned to set financial goals, create a budget, and track her progress against it. She wrote about her experience in a March 2016 article on the *USA Today* website, saying,

> Yes, my student loans have held me back—from saving, investing and having the freedom not to worry about overdrawing my checking account. But I've also gained an awareness of my financial life that will stick with me long after my loans are done dragging me down, an appreciation of the power of liquidity and credit scores and emergency savings that will come in handy when I have far bigger goals in my sights than being able to go to the movies and splurge on fake-buttered, overpriced popcorn.

choice for him. "I graduated from undergrad in 2007 and I graduated from law school in 2010 . . . so I had been in school for a long period of time, had racked up loans from multiple schools and multiple loan programs. I had, probably, 20 loans and eight different lenders by the time that I graduated and I was getting more mail every month that I ever had in my entire life," Foss said in an interview on MarketWatch on January 19, 2016.

"And basically I realized that I couldn't make this many payments every month. I could afford to make a payment but I couldn't cut eight checks every month. And so I went from writing eight checks to one check."

One drawback to loan consolidation is that borrowers can lose benefits offered with their original loans, such as interest rate discounts or loan cancellation benefits. Borrowers considering loan consolidation should think about the potential impact of these changes before consolidating. In his MarketWatch interview, Foss advised college students to evaluate the pros and cons when deciding whether or not to consolidate student loans: "Whenever I'm talking to students I try to get a sense of whether they care most about being able to afford their payment or most about being able to get out from underneath the debt as soon as humanly possible."

When Repayment Difficulties Arise

Sometimes unexpected events can derail a borrower's loan payment plan. Losing a job, developing a serious medical condition, or going through a divorce can all affect a borrower's ability to make loan payments. In these situations of economic hardship, borrowers may be eligible to receive a deferment or forbearance of their student loans. Deferment and forbearance are two ways to postpone the obligation to make payments on student loans. Both can help a borrower through a tough time and avoid defaulting on a loan. In a deferment, the payment of principal and interest on a student loan are temporarily delayed. A forbearance suspends the loan's principal payments but interest still accrues. Unpaid interest is added to the loan's principal balance, increasing the total loan amount.

In some cases, federal student loan debt can be forgiven. Forgiveness of a loan, also called discharge or cancellation, is the release of a borrower's obligation to repay principal and interest on a student loan. Loans can be forgiven if a borrower becomes permanently disabled or dies. They can also be forgiven in exchange for working in the public sector or with certain nonprofit organizations at jobs such as teaching in low-income areas, serving in the military, law enforcement, nursing, working with disabled or high-risk children in low-income communities, and more. Fourth-grade teacher Lori Clarke had $45,000 in student loans forgiven through a South Carolina loan forgiveness program. In exchange for the loan forgiveness, Clarke agreed to work for three years in a high-poverty school near Columbia, South Carolina.

Borrowers who plan to take advantage of loan forgiveness programs should remember that under current tax laws, the amount of a loan forgiven must be reported as taxable income on the borrower's tax return in the year in which the debt is forgiven.

Avoiding Default

When juggling student loan payments with rent, car payments, and other living expenses, some people may be tempted to skip a loan payment or two. However, this can have disastrous financial consequences, putting the loan in default. *Default* means that a borrower has failed to make payments on a student loan as scheduled according to the loan's promissory note, the legal document that the borrower signed when the loan was taken out. The school, government, or institution that made the loan can take action against the borrower to get the money due to them. According to the Consumer

Financial Protection Bureau, nearly 8 million student loan borrowers were in default in 2015, with more than $110 billion in loan balances.

The first day that a borrower misses a payment, the loan becomes delinquent. This lasts until the borrower becomes current on loan payments. Loans that are delinquent for at least ninety days are reported to the three major credit bureaus, giving the borrower a negative credit rating. Defaulting on student loans can leave a significant black mark on a person's credit history, making it harder for him or her to get credit cards, a home mortgage, or a car loan in the future. Additionally, being in default on a student loan will make it very difficult to get additional loans for graduate school.

> "When I first landed in debt, I was so naive. I'll never again brush things under the rug, because I've seen that it will come back to bite me much worse than if I'd faced the situation head-on."
>
> —Kristin Bastian, a financial education manager from North Charleston, South Carolina.

The consequences of student loan default can be devastating. If a borrower defaults on a loan, the loan's entire unpaid balance and accrued interest becomes immediately due. The borrower is no longer eligible to defer the payment or enter certain repayment plans. He or she can lose eligibility for additional federal student aid, and the defaulted loan may be sent to a collection agency. In some cases, the government can request the borrower's employer to withhold money from pay and send it directly to the government for loan repayment. A federal and state tax refund may be withheld to repay defaulted loan debt. Additionally, the loan balance will increase with late fees, interest, collection fees, and other costs related to the collection process.

The Student Aid Bill of Rights

In March 2015 President Barack Obama signed the Student Aid Bill of Rights aimed at helping young adults pay off student loans. The Bill of Rights program is a series of executive directives that are meant to streamline and improve the federal government's interactions with students. It directs the US Department of Education and other federal agencies to make student loan repayments easier. It also proposes that lenders provide better customer service to borrowers and create additional repayment options. Other proposals include rules to require loan collectors to better inform borrowers about repayment options, the design of a new website where students could get all of their loan information in one place, and a website where borrowers could file complaints against lenders. "Every borrower has the right to an affordable repayment plan," Obama said in a March 10, 2015, article on the *USA Today* website. "Every borrower has the right to quality customer service, reliable information, and fair treatment, even if they struggle to repay their loans," he said.

Kristin Bastian, a twenty-nine-year-old financial education manager from North Charleston, South Carolina, graduated in 2009 with $26,500 in student loan debt. Bastian had a hard time finding a job after graduation and took a job as a waitress to pay the bills, including her $200 monthly student loan payment. Money was tight, and paying her student loan was not a priority. She knew that she could call to apply for a deferment or forbearance because of financial hardship, but she felt embarrassed to make the call. "Instead, I pretended my student loans didn't exist," she said in an interview on the *Forbes* website on August 18, 2015.

Then, in 2010, Bastian landed a job for a nonprofit personal finance and housing counseling service with a salary of $28,000. "Even so, I was barely making ends meet—and kept ignoring my loans," she explains. "My wake-up call? When my HR [human resources] manager had to tell me that a collection agency was threatening to garnish my wages and withhold tax refunds. I was forced to sort things out—and it wasn't pretty. My credit score was in ruins (435), and with penalties and accrued interest, I owed significantly more than $26,500 on my student loans," she says. Bastian entered a debt rehabilitation program, which helped her make payments on her loan and repair her credit history. She cautions others against defaulting on student loans: "When I first landed in debt, I was so naive. I'll never again brush things under the rug, because I've seen that it will come back to bite me much worse than if I'd faced the situation head-on."

> "Federal student loans are so flexible that there's always something you can do to make things better. The worst thing someone can do is ignore them."
>
> —Heather Jarvis, a student loan expert.

Keeping on Top of Debt

Paying off student loans can be a long and complicated process. Monthly debt payments can put a strain on a person's finances for years. Without careful management, student loan repayment can quickly get out of hand. "I'd say the most harmful mistake is that some folks are so nervous that they don't address it head-on," said student-loan expert Heather Jarvis in a September 2013 interview on *Forbes*. "Federal student loans are so flexible that there's always something you can do to make things better. The worst thing someone can do is ignore them. I continue to be shocked by how many people are delinquent or in default. And that's just not smart." By understanding how the loans work and the repayment plans available, students can choose the plan that works best for their situation and successfully manage to repay their loans.

Glossary

consolidation: The process of combining one or more loans into a single new loan.

default: The failure to repay a loan according to the terms agreed to in the promissory note.

deferment: A temporary postponement of payment on a loan that is allowed under certain conditions and during which interest does not accrue.

expected family contribution (EFC): The amount that a family is expected to contribute toward education costs.

federal work-study: A federal student aid program that provides part-time employment while a student is in school to help pay education expenses.

financial aid offer: The total amount of financial aid (federal and nonfederal) a student is offered by a college or career school.

financial need: The difference between the cost of attendance at a school and the expected family contribution.

forbearance: A period during which monthly loan payments are temporarily suspended or reduced but interest continues to accrue.

grant: Financial aid, often based on financial need, that does not need to be repaid.

interest: A loan expense charged for the use of borrowed money and calculated as a percentage of the unpaid balance of the loan.

loan: Borrowed money that must be repaid with interest.

merit-based aid: An award that is based on a student's skill or ability.

need-based aid: An award that is based on a student's financial need.

principal: The total amount of money borrowed plus any unpaid interest added to the balance.

private loan: A nonfederal loan made by a lender such as a bank, credit union, state agency, or school.

scholarship: Money awarded to students based on academic, athletic, or other achievements to help pay for education expenses.

subsidized loan: A loan based on financial need for which the federal government pays the interest that accrues while the borrower is in school.

unsubsidized loan: A loan for which the borrower is fully responsible for paying the interest even while still in school.

For More Information

Books

Kalman A. Chany, *Paying for College Without Going Broke*. Natick, MA: Penguin Random House, 2015.

Kristina Ellis, *Confessions of a Scholarship Winner: The Secrets That Helped Me Win $500,000 in Free Money for College—How You Can Too!* Brentwood, TN: Worthy, 2013.

Mark Kantrowitz and David Levy, *Filing the FAFSA: The Edvisors Guide to Completing the Free Application for Federal Student Aid*. Las Vegas: Edvisors Network, 2014.

Lynnette Khalfani-Cox, *College Secrets for Teens: Money Saving Ideas for the Pre-College Years*. Mountainside, NJ: Advantage World, 2014.

Glen Tanabe and Kelly Tanabe, *The Ultimate Scholarship Book 2016: Billions of Dollars in Scholarships, Grants, and Prizes*. Belmont, CA: Supercollege, 2015.

Websites and Online Tools

College Board (www.collegeboard.org). In addition to providing all sorts of college application information, this website has handy online tools for finding scholarships and financial aid, for calculating college costs, and more.

Consumer Financial Protection Bureau (www.consumerfinance.gov). This website offers information about paying for college, including information about student financial aid, loans, comparing financial aid offers, and repaying student loan debt.

Federal Student Aid (https://studentaid.ed.gov). Part of the US Department of Education, this website offers a variety of information about the financial aid process, including information about types of aid, how to apply for aid, and loan repayment.

Finaid (www.finaid.org). This website guides students through financial aid questions with information about a variety of topics, including grants, scholarships, loans, and the aid application process.

Free Application for Federal Student Aid (FAFSA) (https://fafsa.ed.gov). This website from the US Department of Education has information about the FAFSA and its filing process and deadlines.

Saving for College (www.savingforcollege.com). This website features information about savings options for college, tools and calculators, and other information to help students and families plan for college.

Student Loan Calculator (www.bankrate.com/calculators/college-planning/loan-calculator.aspx). This calculator will help students estimate monthly payments and figure out how long it will take them to pay off student loans.

StudentLoans.gov (https://studentloans.gov). This website, sponsored by the Department of Education, has information about student loan programs, repayment options, and the financial aid process.

Index